TANGO

TANGO

Isabel Muñoz & Évelyne Pieiller

Translations from French and Spanish by
Rosanna M. Giammanco-Frongia

Stewart, Tabori & Chang

New York

Production Editor:
Catherine Laulhère-Vigneau

Graphic Design:
Federico del Barrio
Alfonso Meléndez
Jesús Moreno

Reproductions:
Juan Manuel Castro
Mario Parralejo

Photoengraving:
Panchro

Translations from the French and Spanish by
Rosanna M. Giammanco-Frongia, Ph.D.

First published in 1994 by Éditions Plume, 28, rue de Sévigné,
75004 Paris, France

Published in 1997 and distributed by Stewart, Tabori & Chang,
a division of U.S. Media Holdings, Inc., 575 Broadway, New York,
NY 10012

Distributed in Canada by General Publishing Company Ltd.,
30 Lesmill Road, Don Mills, Ontario, M3B 2T6, Canada

Distributed in Australia and New Zealand by Peribo Pty Ltd.,
58 Beaumont Road, Mount Kuring-gai, NSW 2080, Australia

Distributed in all other territories by Grantham Book Services Ltd.,
Isaac Newton Way, Alma Park Industrial Estate,
Grantham, Lincolnshire, NG31 9SD, England

Library of Congress Catalog Card Number: 96-71635

ISBN: 1-55670-597-2

Printed in France

THANKS FOR EVERYTHING...

*I wish to thank all the friends who helped me make this book. I could not have
done it without their art, support, and patience.*

Thanks to the tango dancers Alicia, Orlando and Claudio
Barneix, Claudia Mendoza and Nestor, Claudia Lavalle and
Gabriel Lopards, Luis Castro and Verónica Rodriguez, Pablo
Ojeda and Beatriz Romero, not to mention my Spanish dancers
Paloma Ortiz, Roberto Álvarez, Tony Escartín and Yolanda
García.
To Hector Gabetta and Roberto Ervin, who opened the doors of
Buenos Aires to me.
To Jorge Lebedev, who helped me choose the tangos for this
book.
To my friends Chantal Cottard, Lori Gross, Amador Toril,
Ramón Mourelle, and Moises Santiago.
Finally, a special thanks to Rafael Morès, who first encouraged
me to work on the tango.

To Christian Caujolle, my agent, and the entire VU agency for
their professional know-how and dedication.

And thanks to all the readers who are holding this book in their
hands.

These photos were born even before I took them...
When my parents, when I was a child, adored each other and
adored me, and danced listening to tango music.
Those images were etched in my memory, and I try today to find
them again in this book dedicated to the tango and to the
memory of my parents.

Isabel Muñoz

THE PUBLISHER ALSO WISHES TO THANK...

Éditions P.O.L. for their invaluable *Tango* anthology published
in 1988, produced by Henri Deluy and Saúl Yurkievich, and
those who helped us find again the memory of the songs that
appear in this book.

TABLE OF CONTENTS

Translations from French and Spanish by
Rosanna M. Giammanco-Frongia

PREFACE

Christian Caujolle

BORGES DID NOT LOVE THE TANGO. When he referred to it as a "brothel lizard," he simply forgot to mention that this torrid dance, born in the bordellos of Buenos Aires, in a neighborhood where sailors picked fights with *gauchos*, had made its way into the bourgeois drawing rooms. Most likely he would have been astonished to see how popular this dance has become all over the world, how widely it is being taught and learned, how it modernizes its steps following the wailing of the *bandoneón*, and he might have moderated his disapproval had he been able to witness a small miracle last December, on an improvised stage, one holiday evening, under the glass roof of the old Winter Circus in Buenos Aires. The newspaper *Clarín*, launching a new version of its arts and entertainment section, had assembled three artists: at the piano, an Argentine rock star; on the floor, a young star dancer of the Teatro Colón; and at the microphone, a very old, full-voiced tango singer, who once sang with Carlos Gardel. When, after fifteen magical minutes, the old singer bowed his good-bye and the young dancer took him by the waist to help him exit the stage, the emotion was immense, and several minutes had to pass before the audience dared to applaud. For here was the soul of this rhythm in 2/4 time that suddenly catches fire, speaks of coupling, suddenly suspends desire at the zenith of tension, and starts again on a path firmly set by the male partner.

Put into images, this dance often disappeared behind the conventions that retained only the most visibly dramatic excesses or postures, such as when the bodies stop just short of the kiss, rejected and inevitable at the same time. As with most popular dances, the attempt was made to stereotype the tango as coming from folklore. It was even more difficult to attack this tourist-brochure image, since photography does not show sounds or changes in rhythm, and struggles incessantly against time as it unfolds movement. Yet, Isabel Muñoz has succeeded in expressing the tango, in giving it a voice, in giving it back the restrained desire and the moment of surrender. Whether in a

Buenos Aires alley or in a salon, later in a studio, couples embrace, take a few steps, stop, then start again in the opposite direction. Each time the photograph situates them in space, then attempts to capture the pressure of the hand on a hip, the folds of a 1930s split skirt, the garter suspender holding a fishnet stocking and uncovering a band of milk-white skin, full buttocks that stretch and almost split the fabric of a tight skirt, or the overlapping of two bodies joined as if for eternity. It is thanks to these details, recovering in these images the graphic correspondences of dance's rhythm, that Isabel Muñoz captures the variations and emotions of the tango. A dance becomes form and matter—this is how well the platinum prints evoke the confrontation of fabric and flesh, the rhythmic movements of muscles and material. In brief, the tango comes down to the streaked sole of a high-heeled pump or the small satin bow adorning the strap of a raised slipper, resting on the male dancer's thigh, like time suspended, translating eroticism while recalling the purity of the movement.

The tango is nothing more than a struggle of abstractions answering each other's echoes, lights that reveal each detail of a body in the russet-bronze tone of platinum salts set on paper. A slightly less orange-hued color than the color called "tango" and which Aragon loved to associate with embroidery.

THE GHOST OF QUEENS PAST

Évelyne Pieiller

YOU THINK I'VE HAD too much to drink. You are wrong, Ma'am. I am going to drink now. I get quite interesting when I've had too much to drink. I can spin such lovely tales that you will always regret not having lived them. Then you'd never forget me again.

Am I going to get my beer, or am I going to get kicked out?

You hesitate.

Don't you want to listen to my beautiful tales, my tales of days gone by? No offense intended, Ma'am, but what else do you have to do?

I know it's always like this at this time of night, you are bored because this is the time when men are sad, they don't want to go home because they have nothing at home, no woman, no children, what, kids?— they just have a bed, a TV, a razor, one or two pictures; right, the kids, the razor, once in a while you ask yourself, wouldn't it be worth it to give yourself a good, sharp stroke to the throat, it would make such nice drops of blood on the dirty little shaving mirror. Now then, Ma'am, this is what happens when you can no longer bear growing old alone in polyester suits that you take once a month to the dry cleaner's. But of course, you know all that. Are you giving me this beer, so I can continue to entertain you? What, do I scare you? Have no fear, I am a ghost. You are surrounded by ghosts, Madame. The men who loiter here, even the men we hear playing pool in the back room, are ghosts trying not to disappear completely. Help us, Ma'am. They drag their feet over the cigarette butts on your floor tiles, they have lines around their mouths, and they wear no wedding ring. And they try not to cry. Because, Ma'am, they don't understand what's become of them. Because they've bungled everything. Thank you, Ma'am. Here, this time it's on me. Do not sigh, Ma'am, this man, a storyteller, is now going to entertain you. Yes, of course. Ah, when you frown you remind me of my mother, you get mad just like she did when I was little and didn't stay in bed. She would get mad without saying a word, and my heart would break. When I was little. It no longer affects me that way.

You've seen it, night has fallen outside. And it's starting to drizzle. The light from the street lamps is always more attractive when it rains. Wait, a woman is passing by. No, of course I'm not a magician, I can hear her heels clicking. She's in a hurry, she knows where she's going. She is going home, her son is waiting to have dinner with her. Most likely. Yes, she *was* pretty.

All of sudden it's so quiet.

She is gone. The only noise now is the rain and the billiard balls. Only the rain and the billiard balls can be heard now. And a match lighting up a cigarette. Look, the weather is turning nasty, the sea must be dark down below. You are right to shut the door. Better to be amongst ourselves. And everyone appreciates the sound the rain makes on the windowpanes. Another beer, if you please. When I was a little boy, I was always hoping it would rain. So her lover wouldn't come. My mother's. Don't go, I am talking to you, Ma'am. What are you going to do in the other room? Follow the game? Now that's an idea, I'll escort you. No? So then, you are going to stay and listen to me. My mother was a queen. Like you, perhaps, Madame. Anyway, she was a brunette like you. Her hair was pulled back impeccably, and she wore very sheer stockings, the way they used to wear them back then. Thank you for staying. But that's not why she was a queen. It was the way she carried herself. Like she was immortal. In the neighborhood people called her the Mistress. Me, I used to tell her I would never leave her. Do you have a son, Ma'am? Listen carefully then, I'll tell you a sad secret. When I was little, I wanted to touch her cheeks, my

mother's cheeks. To make her smile. The Mistress never smiled. But she didn't care for it. I would place my hand on her cheek and she would avoid me. She would turn the other way. She would sit up. It gave me a taste like blood in my throat. Like when her lover came. She always thought I was asleep. She would approach my cot, wearing a dress that hugged her hips, like wet fabric, she had on her shiny high heels, she would bend over my cot and turn off the light, sleep, my little one, and would leave the room. When she opened the door I would see the light outside, and then I would plunge in the dark, with just a beam of light framing the door, and I was lonely to the depth of my bones. I would wait. And wait. Please, Lady, another beer.

You are lucky you have an empty lot right across from your establishment. This must surely be the last vacant lot in town. I think I can make out an open fire, way at the end with someone at the side. A hobo. Or maybe two lovers. Has your son ever wanted to stroke your cheek, Ma'am, to make you smile? Please don't get mad. The fire is orange. Under the rain the night is almost white. Have you noticed? Relaxing to look at. There's a good feeling to it. Am I right? Yes, a good feeling, and also sadness. Right after I finish telling you my stories, when I will push the door and leave all shivering, right then we'll be drowning.

Ah, nice stroke in the other room. The ball tapped the other two balls gently. That's hard to do. They've got a good technique in there. We could always go in there, no? The ball tapped them ever so gently, but firm. Very nice.

And the lady leaves again.

Are you going to check the time, or maybe the seam on your stockings? Sorry.

Yes, we'll be drowning. Just an expression, Ma'am. They'll find our solitude all set in our bodies, like a block of cement ready to set. Instantly. Just another way of saying it. In any case, it's good not to a have a clock in here. You show a great understanding in our regard, Madame. In any case, there's still time. Right now I'm talking about my mother. This is always good for ghosts. It makes their pulse quicken, even if they all hide it. Talking about their mother. But no, I am not trying to pick a fight, compose yourself, Sir, I beg you. I said nothing offensive. I simply said we are all trying to look like men. Not like sons. Is there something else now? Maybe I didn't make myself quite clear. Or perhaps I should talk only about myself. It this better now? It took

me a long time before I could realize that I also had a future, not just a past. I don't even really know if I have really grasped this. I talk and talk, but nothing more. I say foolish things. But just to kill time. You know how it is. Thanks, friend, for the beer. Are you leaving? Don't you want to play a game of pool when the table is available? Another time, maybe. Yes, that's it.

No music in here Ma'am? Is there a jukebox where I can put some change? This way we won't hear the pool players, and the squeaking of the chalk as the game proceeds. After a while it becomes irritating.

No. Fine.

The street is totally empty.

Is there really no way, Ma'am? Just so I could stop listening to myself? I'll show you some exotic dances. To warm us up. We get cold easily, we do.

And yet I hear something, vaguely. At intervals. Maybe you left the radio on in the kitchen? So that's why... No, they are having a party down below. With this rain, I wager there aren't too many people. From here, it almost sounds like a barrel organ, wouldn't you say?

It would appear that nothing I say is of any interest to you, dear Lady.

So, no music here. Too bad.

At my mother's, a long time ago, there was music every Saturday. As soon as my door was shut, are you at least following me, Ma'am? I would hear the entrance door open. It was her lover. How would you want me to call him? He would place his hand on my mother's waist. On the wet-looking fabric. With her skin underneath. My mother's. She would take his hand and kiss it. He would wear a signet ring. Which he would later remove. Her eyelids were lowered, and it was exactly as if she were smiling. I would push the door ajar, I couldn't see everything. I could only see a corner, when they crossed my field of vision. A field of vision... Ah, Madame, I would get such a headache from wanting so badly to see and not to see. Didn't you tell me you have a son? You have the same nape as my mother, Ma'am. She would disappear, I would hear the music, I would see them pass again dancing. Without a smile. This was worse. I would see her hand on his thigh. And the music. Just a glimmer of music. Me, I stood between darkness and light. All my body was in darkness, and my eyes were bathed in light. With my nails driven in the wall plaster. She would place her leg on his thigh. When they danced, they seemed not to move. They did

not utter a word. They didn't look at each other. They rent air as if slashing it in two. I would look at the man's hands. On her waist, my mother's waist. In the hollow, where it's soft. Where everything is hidden. And the glimmer of music. With the needle scratching the worn-out record.

It's my treasure.

My mother, not looking at the man, only has eyes for him. Her heels are on the ground. She raises her thigh. The fabric makes a noise at it falls back. The small *bandoneón*. The man's hand flat and secure in the hollow. And my mother bends, stretches, tangles her legs, leans on her stomach.

My treasure.

I would look. Her skin glowed. I would look. She didn't see me. She would lean back in the man's arms. The music cut through you like a knife stabbing. She would lean back. Oh, Sir. You are leaving. I hope I wasn't boring you. One more minute, if you please. Appreciate the ways in which we are similar. Do you concur, Madame? A striped suit, a hat, a signet ring, and both of us skinny as alley cats. May I offer you one last glass, or am I keeping you? As you wish.

Your patron does not care for this type of chumminess. It is striking, however. We probably cry at the same scenes when we go to the movies.

But you're not like us, are you Madame? You are not the crying type. You make others cry. I'm talking nonsense. Drunk talk. Kick me out. Now is the time. It stopped raining. It's misty, however. You can't even see the empty lot now, it looks like the sea is right in front. Ah, my friend has been wiped out. Erased. Could be we are the last survivors. Could be everything around us has disappeared, swallowed by whiteness. We are now on an island. Lost at sea. And the distant blare from below is coming from a faraway liner, crossing the sea all aglow, as it disappears into the distance. Without seeing us.

Gentlemen, will someone offer me a cigarette, I don't have any more. Thank you.

I smoked my very first cigarette one Saturday night. I was in my black hole. I had turned my back. I was sitting on the floor, against the door. As if sitting in a pool of blood. The *bandoneón* created a cave for me and I was deep inside it. Alone like a god. With my heart beating in unison with the music. It hurt. I had no thoughts. I was all absorbed by the loud throbbing in my heart. In my hole.

Why am I telling you all this?

Because it's a Saturday night.

Sorry. Cigarettes make me cough.

But there's no music here, you know.

Real music.

The one coming from below is child's play. It lacks feeling. Either that or I'm too old.

Tell me, they do take their time next door to take aim. They are artists. Ma'am, I'm taking my beer to the billiard room. But why is the door shut? The footsteps have stopped.

We are more and more isolated, do you feel that?

And where are these cries coming from?

When the needle scratched against the record player, the footsteps stopped. Me, I got up, left my black hole, crossed the lit area, went to look for a cigarette in my mother's pack and took the gold lighter he always placed next to his signet ring. He looked at me and smiled. My mother was in front of the record player, her nape straight, her dress glued to the hollow of her back. She didn't turn. I lit my cigarette. Let out the smoke. And went back across the space. When the music picked up again, I was leaning against my door looking at the smoke moving up to my hair.

Now where are these cries coming from?

Oh, it's the seagulls.

Or just one seagull?

I hope it stops shrieking.

At that point, I was telling myself that never again would I feel pain.

Such nonsense.

That never again would I love her. I had become celibate. She could dance all she wanted. Her chest leaning against the man. The man's hand on her knee. The thigh raised and the skirt sliding against the silk stocking. All she wanted. She could. Me, I was through with it. I no longer had feelings. She wouldn't look at me when I left the room. Fine. The gold lighter was heavy in my hand. I placed it on my forehead. It felt cool. In the other room the music was playing again. Noise of footsteps, fabric, hands on flesh. Very well. I was elsewhere. Far from her. So far away that I felt like a stranger in my own room.

I'm moving on to cognac, Madame. Have no fear, I will leave the moment I feel my stubble growing. We do have principles, men like me especially.

The mist is getting thicker, it almost looks like snow. Now you can't see anything. Except for the open fire and some party lights. Just barely. Silence everywhere. I'll have to whisper. You'll have no more patrons tonight. Maybe you would like to go and rest awhile. Aren't you ever afraid, Ma'am, all alone here, in this forsaken corner, with drunkards and gamblers? Have you ever had any fights? My cognac, if you would. Thank you, Madame.

Oh, they stopped having fun in the back, you may have noticed, the only noise now is the cue hitting the parquet floor, this is the time of nerves, the best time for lovers of the game, listen.

Those strokes, they are terrible.

And here, all is quiet.

If I stop talking, all is quiet.

Are you a believer; I see, you must forgive me, you are wearing a small cross. Very graceful. Ivory and silver, right? A family heirloom, no doubt. I know it's a bit indiscreet, but don't knit your brows like that, come on, Ma'am, I'm not even asking you at what age you got married.

Oh my God.

A seagull just threw itself against the window.

I really will end up believing we are at sea, motionless like the damned.

I can't take this silence any more.

How can you bear it?

It's a bad silence. A silence that brushes against you. You don't think so? Is everyone OK?

Could it be I am starting to get drunk, maybe?

You really don't find it unsettling not to hear

anything, except me and the footsteps on the parquet floor, the balls gliding, the matches lighting? Me, it makes me nervous.

And still no music, dear Lady?

So then, another cognac.

Would someone like to chat with me? Exchange a few banalities? It's easy. Did someone already go to the amusement park down below? No. Good. It was an example. Now then. We don't have the age any more, that's for sure. We could, however, go with our children. They always have a good time with the haunted house and the house of mirrors. As far as I know. In any case, it seems they are going to get rid of the amusement park. To make room for an office building. Oh well.

Why is the seagull squalling. Ah, this particular species will never become endangered. It's too greedy, you've seen it.

It looks at me at it passes.

With its small round eye.

It looks at me.

Excuse me, it wasn't my intention to startle the company, but I can't stand these animals. I always think they are waiting to pluck out my eyes. Maybe I knocked a bit too hard. Well, at least it's no longer glued to the window.

Ma'am, stop touching your cross right there, where your breasts begin, it's indecent, and talk a while with me. It will change our ideas. No. The mistress of the house is unwilling. She wants to keep her ideas to herself. Now then, I've offended the mistress. I have a propensity for offending people. It's a talent just like any other. A very small talent. But a talent nevertheless. I talk, I babble, I amuse, sometimes I'm even interesting, and so I become offensive. The sting of a hornet. That's all. Or of a varmint. Ah, I've made you smile, Ma'am, fleetingly, but I did it. It's the dream of a lifetime, Ma'am. Yes, yes, I fathomed a smile that went through your body, and your ankles relaxed a bit in your high-heeled shoes.

The fire outside died out.

Not true.

It's as if it's becoming increasingly distant.

More and more unforgettable.

In this field of fog.

You are no longer paying attention, am I right?

You haven't been paying attention for a good while.

My flickering fire outside does not excite you. Beckoning like a lighthouse beacon. Or like the cigarette of a vanished man. Or maybe, even, like a lamp at the entryway of a forbidden place. Oh no, it's back. Why is this damn seagull attracted to this place?—

Sorry, Ma'am.

Another small drink.

Sir, could it be I am making you leave? I *have* been a bit loud. Frankly, however, it's as if we were sitting with a corpse. Look out for yourself. When the night is white, like tonight, it's easy to get lost. To dissolve. Don't you want to stay here, safely behind the windows? He didn't even reply.

Men are sullen, Ma'am. Gloomy and boring like an ill-lit hallway one has taken for years. Which doesn't prevent one from always tripping on the small, last step.

If it comes any closer, this damn seagull, I'll go out and knock her off. I can't stand her tiny round eye.

I don't have to calm down, Ma'am, why should I calm down, I'm scared of seagulls, so what? Aren't *you* afraid of anything, with your spiked heels and your little cross in between your breasts? A rock. A statue. A madonna. Congratulations, Ma'am. Me, I'm not that strong. A cognac, Ma'am, for the man who's scared. Ah, I detect my colleagues are coming out of their thoughts to pay attention to me again. Well, of course I'm scared.

Otherwise why would I be here all alone late at night in this forsaken pub? I've known so many pubs, at night everyone always looks like a skull, thanks to the neon lights. Who would have ever thought, when we were kids, that we would lead this kind of life?

Beat it, you bastard!

In any case, it can't always be the same bird. Please, Ma'am, try not to give me that look. Only one woman had the power to move me, just one, my little lady, and she burned me down to ashes. I wasn't grown yet, and I was ashes. After that, it was over. The emotions. Ah, this, this really makes you laugh. Good. Laugh. Offer me a cigarette for the effort. Come on, laugh.

In other countries, people would think that fire outside is the maw of hell.

After that, I left. For the other end of the world. Yes. I didn't speak my language any more. I didn't wear a hat any more. I changed my first name.

Do I make you dream, gentlemen?

All I did abroad was grow old.

I just grew old. I saw countrysides, women, factories, cities, policemen, hobos. So what... Like everyone else. More? More of what? I saw dancing halls as big as hangars, and fireworks in the gardens of white castles. Yes.

I even saw a city burn. More? No, enough of that. Look. I stretch out my arms and hit the Formica top, like this! I make the windowpanes shake, and the mistress gives a start. Always. Just like when I was abroad. And, like then, the mistress, ah the mistress doesn't believe one word of my stories. In a nutshell, gentlemen, it's always like this. Isn't it so, my fair lady? Not a word. She doesn't believe I flung my underwear, the gold lighter and my prize books into a suitcase. No, of course not. She doesn't believe that before I left I broke my mother's spiked heels. Gentlemen, she won't even believe that my mother wrote to me. Hundreds of miles from here. No. She is not interested. What would you have written your son, had he run away from you? Come back? Do not come back?

What? Ah... all of this.

Every Saturday night she danced. Did I tell you already?

Except when it rained.

I never understood why, but when it rained he wouldn't come.

She danced. It wasn't too long ago, you understand that. Maybe, let's see, fifteen years. Twenty. Maybe even thirty years.

What age would you say I am, Ma'am?

Difficult for me to conceive that I'm older today than my mother was when she danced. So, what would you have told your son if he had left home? You can click your heels and go to the back room, I know you are listening to me. One cognac, Madame, one, if you please. And it's not the last one. Very sorry.

Once, I opened my door all the way. Loudly. Like in the westerns. He raised his eyes without stopping. She put her hip forward and closed her eyelids. The artery in my neck was pulsating to the beat of the music. She whispered, go back in, my child, and they turned together, thigh against thigh. I said you stop. They glided together. I cried you stop. She stopped. She turned around. Him, he was now leaning against a wall. She turned towards me. The music continued. She said to me, what's happening with you, my son? I said I want you to come with me. She was sweating at her hair roots, and there was a dark line in between her breasts down to her stomach. She asked me very gently, are you sick, do you have a fever? I started crying. I was a child. I held out my hand to her. I touched her arm lightly, she pulled back. I sat on the floor and went on sobbing. The record had stopped. She told me get up now, and go to bed. I rocked my head on her knees, that night she was wearing fish-net stockings, she touched my forehead, and very low she said to me, yes baby, go. I went back to my bedroom, and when I closed the door the music started again. She whispered, sleep well my son. You approve of this, Ma'am, tell me. Of course, I know, she was right. Her tango and her lover were no concern of mine. Your small cross is moving too fast, you are moved, Mistress, or what, tell me once and for all, that I may finally understand! Are you upset, amused, nervous? Just tired! Oh. I wouldn't have thought one could be so out of breath just by being tired.

I know the changes in breathing. Very well.

To be more exact, you have trouble finding your breath. You are short of breath. Your chest is blocked. Maybe you are even afraid, at this point, of choking. You conceal it as best you can, however it's difficult to hide. I am an expert. Truly, Ma'am, you are exasperated.

I always have this effect on women with a straight nape and hip-hugging dresses. From the time I was a kid, as I told you.

No, no more cognac, thank you.

Would you rather I fall to pieces, tell me, or start stammering, or that I leave on unsteady legs whimpering in my coat collar? Then I would be just one more drunk, Ma'am, totaled like all drunks, they all think they're unique, isn't it lady, but they are all alike, my poor lady, but you have to put up with them, for the sake of business... Dear little lady, from now on I will drink only mineral water. And I won't take pictures out of my wallet. I have no pictures. Stop fidgeting with your cross. It bothers me.

Now we are breathing easier, from what I can see.

She hates me.

It's nothing, mistress. Just a passing customer. As soon as you've seen him, you've forgotten him.

That billiard game is endless. Are you waiting for them to finish before closing? Do you work so hard to pay for your son's fine college studies? It's expensive when there's no father.

Ah, she goes into the kitchen. She's jilting me, the mistress. She has taken offense.

To bear the ineptitude of all these disillusioned men year after year. To not be able to wear slippers, to be compelled to keep your lips good and painted, just when you'd want to remove your makeup and go to sleep, it's a bitch of a job, Ma'am. Did you really think people would take your ring for a wedding band, or you just don't care?

Anyway, this is the bar of the unengaged. Not one of your clients is wearing a wedding ring, dear Madame. This is the life of sad people.

What are you doing in the kitchen? Are you sitting on a chair and have you taken your shoes off? Or are you trying not to think? Especially about me? You've forgotten my mineral water.

Madame, I will talk even if my throat is dry and even if you are not here. I will talk to the mirror on the opposite wall. I'm used to it. The mirror is just a little bit unsteady. Like the ground, in any case. Some cigarette stubs, some rolling paper, and I leave out the rest. It's relaxed in here, Madame.

So, what are you doing?

Come back, I won't vex you any more.

I'll tell you about my travels. I will tell you strange tales. I'll no longer tell you about my little nightmares. You understand? I'll only tell you educational things. How the polar bear lives and why it roams so much. For example. Is this agreeable? Would you like this, Ma'am? Or would you rather I describe the Vienna Opera House? Answer me. What is it that can relax you? London fashions, raising crocodiles in Australia, lepers at the entrance of African hotels, the Oktoberfest in Munich? Please smile. Even if you smile from afar, I will know. Nothing? Still nothing. Stop burrowing yourself in the kitchen. Maybe you feel sick? Do you need any help?

She's as immovable as bronze.

I bet you're crying.

She cries standing, in the dark, her fists tight, her eyelids tightly closed to keep from crying, but she is crying nevertheless. Why? Because of everything.

It's strange how for a long time we say to ourselves, one day things will change, everything will be better, it will happen, and then little by little we no longer say it to ourselves. It's over. We no longer believe.

Look, the wind must have shifted. Ah, this is wonderful, I can hear real music, Ma'am, our music, it must have come back into fashion. Ah, this is music to dance to, to hold each other too tightly in a corner and to cry to on the roller coaster; it almost makes me happy. It grips the heart. Like when we see snow at Christmas time, there are wreaths, and we have been forgotten. Luckily, none of this concerns us any more. Our chest hairs are turning gray. And we'll no longer hurt anyone. We've learned to live all alone. Like grownups. Ma'am? We don't talk love to anyone. We are correct. Ma'am? We get by in our furnished rooms.

Ma'am?

It's over already. Just time for a sigh, after all. Why can't this damn seagull fly into the fire, why can't it leave us alone, so we won't talk about it any more!

Nothing, Ma'am, just the seagull who again tried to kill itself by throwing itself against the window. Your last patron is gone to sleep. He'd rather sleep here. My God. Do you know him? Answer me, go on. Are you afraid your voice will come out all choked up? Very important. There's only the two of us left. And the pool players next door. My voice is also hoarse. Do tell me, do you know him? He must be even lonelier than me.

You did notice, when I shut up it's even worse. Silence could wake him up.

You love that guy a lot, I can tell. I must admit he's no trouble at all. You must also despise him a little. Oh, very well, excuse me. So then, you must be afraid of him. Did he talk to you before? Do you ever ask yourself if one day it could come to that? No. Of course. To sleep with one's head on a slightly sticky table, under neon lights. Could be a solution, after all. But really a last resort.

Is it time for a cigarette, Madame? Could you offer me one, with no hard feelings? One could almost believe we appreciate each other

if we smoke a cigarette together. The two smokes blend, look Madame, they stretch, they find each other again, you can no longer tell which is which. You're already finished?

He's dreaming. It's a little disgusting.

What would you have written to your son, Ma'am if he had left home? I need you? Live your life, I am proud of you? What? Give me your point of view.

The mist is clearing up. Maybe we'll finally be able to tell who's standing by the fire. There is someone by the fire, isn't there? With this flickering neon, I feel as if I am hallucinating. Your lamp is soon going to crack, Ma'am.

What a deep sigh. You'd rather I leave. I'm like a hanger-on, dear lady. You don't have to put the mop all over my ankles, I understand. You resent the fact that I know you were crying just now.

The sleeper is still moving.

Were you thinking you'd never leave this pub, that you'd spend all your nights here, your nape straight, your ankles swollen? You could always say that's what life is.

Stop with that mop, my pant cuffs are all wet.

But is this really what life is?

Oh, very nice.

You smooth your dress over your hips with the same care you'd use to brush your brows.

Now that's class, Madame.

The fog is going to get inside, what are you doing? And you'll catch cold if you stand outside. But that's what you want. As you wish. That's the kind of effect I have on you.

The lady is smoking. On the other side.

Look at me. Our profiles are ten feet apart. Our stiff profiles. Ten feet and a door. You won't look at me.

Do you intend to lower the shutters? If you want, I could wake up the sleeper. Unless he's dead. Ah! I was sure the sorry bitch would get in, sooner or later. It's going to tear into our hair and pluck our eyes out. Help me, I'm telling you, seagulls pluck the eyes out, help me instead of laughing, and this guy, why doesn't he wake up, get a mop, I'll take the broom, do what I do, keep your eyes covered, ah, look, it got all tangled up in the bottles, chase it out, good God, yeah, out the door, there, what are you waiting for, she'll break a window, careful, there you've got it, bravo!

I thought it was going to get up into your hair. Are you OK? No scratches? My hands are still shaking.

I'll help you clean up. All this glass on the floor, it's dangerous. The guy's still sleeping, look at him, he's in a coma. There's really glass all over. And feathers. On top of that, I just cut myself. Why in the world did you leave the door open? With that fog, it's so white it's like being blind already. You didn't have to go out, you could have just asked me to leave. Are you asking me to now? Pass me the broom. And take care of that guy. Maybe he passed out. I'll clean up the glass and after, I promise, you'll be rid of me, I'll go home. My home. *Chez moi. A la casa.* Warm and familiar, the way it should be. But you don't care. You just don't care. That I am all alone. And that I cry. But no, Ma'am, I am like you, I never cry. A tough guy. A real man. Or almost. We know how to swallow our sobs. Down to the plexus.

Look at it, I'm dripping blood. I really cut myself. There, the palm. It's nothing. It does bleed however. Give me the cognac, I'll staunch the cut, otherwise I'll drip blood all over the place. Try not to slip, especially, sorry, I've got stains all over you. Would you have a piece of cloth so I can bandage it? No, not this Ma'am, it's too soft, it looks like silk. You have nothing else? A piece of rag? Thanks. I'm complicating things. It seems they are calling for you, in the back room. No? I thought I heard cues. Thanks. That's fine. Your lamp is going to crack. It's not a drop in electricity.

Where did the guy go?

Maybe we better call a doctor.

Would you like me to lend a hand?

I can see you are used to it. The water bucket technique, although well known, is still highly effective. Won't he be mad when he wakes up? He's half choking, look. Oh, the cut is open again, the cloth is soaked, if you'll allow me, I'll go get a saucer to avoid spilling blood all over.

Good-bye, friend.

Well, that was quick. When you make a decision things happen quickly. He was totally soaked, the poor guy. Does he do this regularly? And he never gets mad? Aging men are strange creatures, Madame. And what's more, he keeps coming back. He has great faith in you, Madame. True, it's the faith of the drunk. And the pool players, are they deaf or what?

You could get slaughtered, they wouldn't move. Obviously, I still can't go in there. No. Why not? It's not a striptease joint. In any case, if that were the case, it would certainly be advisable for me to go. I am a male patron, of legal age, and most certainly unattached, Ma'am. I have a telephone at home, you

realize that. What a joke. After all however, I do have a mailbox, so why not the phone also?

My hand's still bleeding.

The bird's come back. It's flying around the fire. It's a crazy bird. I always thought seagulls were crazy. I am all white, so, possibly, what conclusion do you draw? I am losing blood my dear little lady, this has never helped anyone look fresh and rosy like the fairy tale princesses. You have a little mark on your neckline, like a beauty mark. Very coquettish. It's a real mess in here. I'll help you clean up. Now that it's bleeding less. I'm asking myself what it is that got cut. The nuisance is that as soon as I move, the cut reopens. Ah, the billiard balls are starting up again. Men are impassive. Once upon a time I used to play a mean game of pool.

Look at that. You're treating yourself to a little cognac to recover from all these emotions. Very selfish. Me, I could bleed to death, nothing. No thanks, no cognac for me. Is it too much to ask for coffee? Let's drink, Madame. To the damage.

This feels good.

The night is almost over.

I was in a place like this, but on the other side of the world, when I decided to go back home.

Except there was a jukebox. I was wearing silk stockings then. I was reading the paper, everyone was quiet as in a family boarding house. The mistress of the place was wearing butterfly-shaped glasses. Once in a while a patron would get up to play a record. Always the same. No one complained. He kept the music low. In any case, there was no conversation. It came to me suddenly. I couldn't explain it. I folded the paper. I took out my wallet. The song was playing. I felt the bones in my fists. Did this ever happen to you? You would have to tell about that, Ma'am, we are chatting away, nothing more, nothing more. It's still allowed by law. Oh, a tiny smile, so tiny.

I kept turning the lighter's striker wheel. Outside, at that moment, a woman was passing by fast, her hands in her pockets. I decided to go home. Even before I knew what my thoughts were, it was a done deal. So tell me, why can't I go in the back room? What's going to happen if I go anyway? Are they going to break my neck? Should I phrase it more elegantly, or is this enough? Who's going to break my neck? Ma'am, I'm finally going to dream.

The seagull is perching now. Yes, all the way in the back, next to the fire. White on white,

not easy to make out, clearly. It's the white that's moving about. It's rearranging its wing. It's going to sleep.

What time do you close?

Ah, the lady is gone again.

Me, I stay put like an idiot. All alone. With the smell of cold cigarette butts and stale beer. With my back to the mirror. I must go home to sleep. Men, isn't it, Ma'am, luckily they don't cry.

Here we are again.

I was already missing you. I missed you, I miss you, I will miss you, Madame, but let it go.

Don't they ever stop? How can you stand this noise the whole night long? The balls, the feet, the chalk on the table to mark the points, the tension of it all. My God. Who's winning?

By the way, do you know what your sleeper is doing right this minute?

He's sleeping in his bed, fully dressed, and he's looking straight ahead.

I'm going.

How much do I owe you?

You will *not* get old.

Do you know this? Do you?

You won't get old. Because you live all inside. Yourself. You keep yourself in a dark, golden chamber, with closed windows, good and straight on your slim heels, the stockings turning well around your legs, the dress good and tight on your stomach, your cross between your breasts, and so, you wait. The nape erect, you eyes lowered. Everything else bothers you. What you do here, the people, and when you have to talk.

Oh, how you are listening to me.

In your dark, golden chamber, you are absent from everything else, and you lie waiting. When the man places his hand on your body, Madame, you are his queen, and you are a queen to yourself. Isn't it so, Madame. You only want the expectation, and leave the rest to slip away, and you always feel with certainty your hair fall with all its weight down to the hollow in your back, isn't is so Madame, even when you keep it tightly wound up in a neat bun. Thank you for not telling me that you don't understand a thing about what I am saying, Madame.

Thank you for raising your head and looking me straight in the eyes.

And yet you can't slap me.

I am the man who can sneak a red flower in between your breasts. From a distance. Just by forcing you to think. Sweet, red petals between your breasts.

Would you be so kind as to pass me another saucer? This one is going to overflow. You know bleeding is very good for you. In the ports I used to sail to, a long time ago, they would do it often. It was like a cleansing. To pick up one's spirits again. I already feel better. I feel better in my bones. That's it. The neon light makes everything disjointed.

Aren't you changing the fuses? You'd rather stay in the dark? How about your friends in the back room? How can they continue their game? You should go and check.

The only noise left is the refrigerator. And myself. And your heels.

Before I went abroad, just before I left, one Saturday night, when my mother told me to go on to bed, I said no, stay with me. Once. Let's go for a walk. Have fun with me, once. She sat on a Formica chair and she said, why now?

It's really dark in here, Madame. But it's much better. In the back they lit some candles. The door is framed by a slender tremulous light, and we are in the dark. The neon was hurting my eyes. This is restful. We are in the dark. The blood is dripping much more slowly.

I replied I was her son. After all. She thought about it. We both stood there in the waning day. Do you understand, Madame, when I tell you I have never been happier since.

When it was almost night, I was sleeping with my eyes open, I was almost sleeping, that's how calm I was, she got up, she smoothed her dress with her hand, and said, fine. She went to get a coat and I raised my eyes. Framed by the door I saw the man; he bowed slightly, and in raising his hat made a half-turn. My mother and I left. For a walk. She was smoking. I really didn't know where to take her. We went to see the ships. And I understood she was getting bored. I was thirteen. I lit her cigarettes with the gold lighter. I told her she was beautiful. That's all. I didn't know what to say to her. I ended up by asking her if I could smoke. She didn't want me to. We sat on a bench, it was starting to get chilly, and she put her arm around my shoulders and said, when I was young, before you were born, I wanted to leave. Just like that. I don't know why. To be somewhere else. To know things. To leave. To go to the other side. And so I told her, let's do it. Now. You are not old. Now.

Luckily there's a fire out there. With this mist and the darkness in here, one could easily get a sick feeling.

Tell me who's in the other room. Look, what's it going to do to you, I am leaving. Are they gambling for money? Are they transvestites? Are they cops? Come on… Your lover? Your child? I can barely see you, they won't get upset in any case. I am telling you about my little life, you could at least answer me. Or maybe there is nothing. Only a recorded tape. Only your memories. I said to her I'll take you away. We'll manage. All you have to do is handle the paperwork. And things will be different there. She was smoking. She didn't reply. We were looking out to the sea. We were frozen. I insisted; my teeth were starting to chatter. She stood up and without looking at me she told me I can't, come, let's go home. I should have done this earlier, now this is how things are, come on, let's go. Ah, you, Madame, you certainly know what she must have been thinking of, my mother, as she stood shivering in the cold.

Well, after all, what does it matter?

You still haven't told me how much I owe you.

Are you still there?

Soon it will be the time when serious-minded people will stretch their hand to stop the alarm. And my stubble is starting to itch. I am releasing you, Madame. Write up my check and I'll leave. I'll make believe I leave my house to go get the bus, and wait for the day to be over. Ma'am? The backroom door is open. It's empty. They left. They left. If you will allow me to bring you a candle. Ah, not bad. I haven't lost my hand. There was even a little record player in a corner.

I'm going, I'm going, don't worry.

It will be good for you to be finally alone.

There is really a figure next to that fire. Is it one of your former patrons? I am going. Are you writing my check?

When we came back home, he was there. His back to the wall, his leg bent back. He was smoking. He smiled at me, and he slapped her. Then he kissed her hand. I rushed on top of him shouting, my mother said don't get involved, he blocked my hands. I cried Mama tell him we are leaving. She opened the door saying what are you talking about, we are staying put, calm yourself. He let go of me. She was already inside. He looked at me. I shouted, I am leaving. She didn't answer. He offered me a cigarette and went in. What I would like to know, Madame, is if later she cried.

Later.

Don't you really want me to pay the bill?

In the candlelight, you are as secret, Madame, as a letter gone astray.

Pay no attention to it, the banknotes are a little stained.

I think the man next to the fire is signaling us, look. He is raising his hand. What is he holding? It seems to be sparkling. It's a crown.

A white iron crown, Madame, he is offering to you.

Why did you blow out the candle? He is now on his knees, you can see better than I, I can no longer make him out.

He is either sobbing, Madame, or crying.

Ah, my sleeve was soaking in this damn saucer.

Madame? Madame?

She's gone.

What if I joined the man by the fire, Madame, to warm up your coffee?

It's dangerous for you to leave me, Madame.

Do you still have your hair in a bun, or are you letting your hair down?

That's a strange way of putting people out the door.

What if I hanged myself. With my fancy tie.

Nothing. Not one sound. Not one sniffing.

We could have gone back, Madame, together.

Do you know what he's doing, down there in the empty lot? He is slowly placing the crown on his head. He's not moving. He's standing. He's lit by the fire.

I'm gone, Madame. The money is on the counter. Madame, I am as happy as I could possibly be.

SILBANDO (1923)

Una calle en Barracas al sud,
una noche de verano,
cuando el cielo es más azul
y más dulzón el canto del barco
italiano...
Con su luz mortecina, un farol
en la sombra parpadea
y en el zaguán
está un galán
hablando con su amor...

Música:
Cátulo Castillo y Sebastían Piana

WHISTLING

A STREET in Barracas, to the south,
on a summer night,
when bluer is the sky
and sweeter is the song
wafting from the Italian boat...
Its light dying, a street-lamp
flickers in the shadows
and underneath a portico
a lover
speaks to his beloved...

Lyrics:
José González Castillo

A NIGHT ON THE TOWN

¡ Garufa !,
pucha que sos divertido.
¡ Garufa !,
ya sos un caso perdido.

Reveler!
Dammit, you're such fun!
Reveler!
A wasted man you are.

Lyrics:
Roberto Fontaina, Víctor Soliño

ESTA NOCHE ME
EMBORRACHO (1928)

FIERA venganza la del tiempo,
que le hace ver deshecho
lo que uno amó...
Este encuentro me ha hecho
tan mal,
que si lo pienso más
termino envenenao.
Esta noche me emborracho bien,
¡ me mamo bien mamao !
pa'no pensar...

Música : *Enrique Santos Discépolo*

TONIGHT, I'M GETTING
DRUNK

HARSH is time's revenge,
for it reveals the ruins
of the one we used to love...
And this encounter's caused me
so much sorrow,
the very thought of it
floods through me like poison.
Tonight I'm getting good and drunk
I'll drink and drink and drink!
So as not to think...

Lyrics : *Enrique Santos Discépolo*

MI NOCHE TRISTE (1917)   MY SAD NIGHT

PERCANTA que me amuraste   WOMAN, you put me in a cage
en lo mejor de mi vida   in the flower of my life,
dejándome el alma herida   my soul left bleeding,
y espinas en el corazón.   a thorn in my heart.
sabiendo que te quería.   And yet you knew I loved you,
que vos eras mi alegría   and that you were my joy,
y mi sueño abrasador: you were my fiery dream;
para mí ya no hay consuelo   now I can find no peace
y por eso me encurdelo   and to forget your love
pa' olvidarme de tu amor.   I must get drunk.

Música : *Samuel Castriota*   Lyrics : *Pascual Contursi*

36

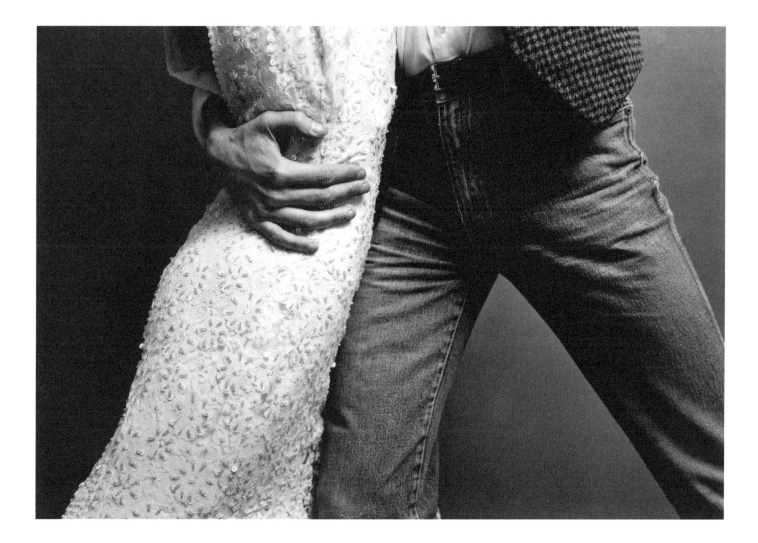

ROSICLER (1946)

ROSE OF DAWN

Te llamabas Rosicler,
como el primer
rayo del día...
Y en los lirios de tu piel
todo mi ayer se perfumó...
Ese ayer que me persigue
con su máscara terrible
de dolor y de imposibles...
Ya me voy... rubia mujer,
yo nunca más
he de volver...

Música : *José Basso*

Your name was Rose of Dawn
like the day's
first ray of light...
My yesteryears were scented
in the lilies of your skin...
Those yesteryears now haunt me,
with their dreadful mask
of sorrow and futility...
Now I leave... my fair woman,
never more
shall I return...

Lyrics: *Francisco García Giménez*

¡ Y todo a media luz,
qué brujo es el amor !
A media luz los besos,
a media luz los dos.
Y todo a media luz,
crepúsculo interior.
¡ Qué suave terciopelo
la media luz de amor !

Música : *Edgardo Donato*

IN A HALF LIGHT

THE half-light where we meet,
bewitches us with love,
a half-light shades our kisses,
a half-light from above.
My twilight here with you,
is in a half-light too.
A smooth and gentle velvet
is the half-light of our love.

Lyrics : *Carlos César Lenzi*

EL CHOCLO (1947)

Por tu milagro de notas agoreras.
nacieron sin pensarlo las paicas y
las grelas.
luna en los charcos. canyengue en
la caderas
y un ansia fiera en la manera
de querer...

Al evocarte...
tango querido...
siento que tiemblan las baldosas
de un bailongo
y oigo el rezongo de mi pasado.
Hoy que no tengo...
más a mi madre...
siento que llega en punta 'e pie
para besarme
cuando tu canto nace al son
de un bandoneón.

Música :
Angel Gregorio Villoldo

AN EAR OF CORN

By the miracle of your prophetic
notes women and girls were
instantly born,
moonlight in water pools,
their hips born to sway
and a wild longing
in their way of loving...

When I think of you,
beloved tango...
I feel the tiles
of the dance hall shake
and hear the moaning of my past.
Today I don't have...
my mother any more...
but I feel her coming
on tiptoes to kiss me,
when your song springs
from the sound of the bandonéon...

Lyrics: *Enrique Santos Discépolo,*
Juan Carlos Marambio Catán

TOMO Y OBLIGO (1931)

Si los pastos conversaran esta
pampa le diría
con qué fiebre la quería, de qué
modo la adoré.
Cuántas veces de rodillas,
tembloroso,
yo me he hincado
bajo el árbol deshojado donde un
día la besé.

Siga un consejo, no se enamore
y si una vuelta le toca hocicar,
fuerza, canejo, sufra y no llore
que un hombre macho no debe
llorar.

Música: *Carlos Gardel*

THIS ROUND'S ON ME

If pastures could speak
this pampa would tell you
with what passion I loved her,
how truly I worshipped her.
How often
trembling on my knees,
have I stood beneath the leafless tree
where one day I'd kissed her.

Take my advice, don't fall in love,
but if one day
you should fall on your face,
be strong, my man,
suffer without crying
'cause real men don't cry.

Lyrics: *Manuel Romero*

AMARGURA (1934)

BITTERNESS

ME persigue implacable
su boca que reía.
Acecha mis insomnios
ese recuerdo cruel.
Mis propios ojos vieron
cómo ella le ofrecía
el beso de sus labios,
rojos como un clavel.

Un viento de locura
atravesó mi mente.
Deshecho de amargura
yo me quise vengar.
Mis manos se crisparon,
mi pecho las contuvo,
su boca que reía
yo no pude matar.

Música : *Carlos Gardel*

HER laughing mouth
relentlessly pursues me.
A merciless memory
that stalks my sleepless nights.
My own eyes have seen her
offer him a kiss,
from her
carnation-red lips.

A wild wind of folly
raged through my mind.
I bitterly sought
revenge for my pain.
My hands contracted,
my heart restrained them,
her laughing mouth
I could not bear to kill.

Lyrics: *Alfredo Le Pera*

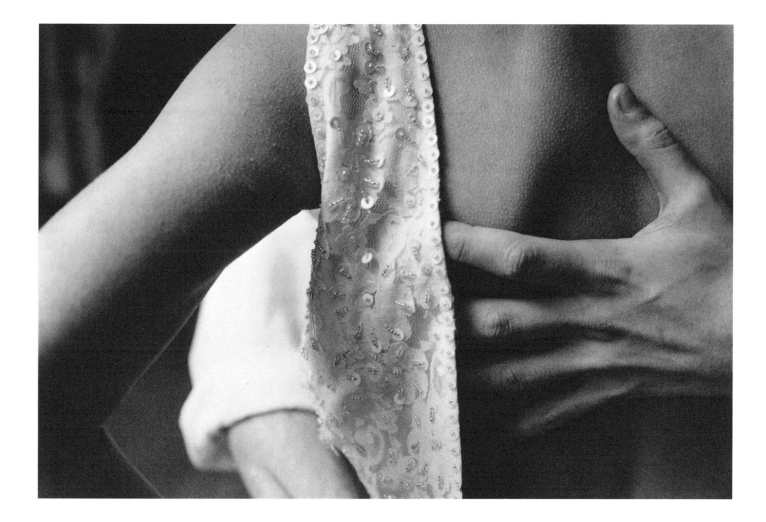

NINGUNA (1942)

NO ONE

No habrá ninguna igual.
Niguna con tu piel ni con tu voz.
Tu piel, magnolia que mojó la luna.
Tu voz, murmullo que entibió el
amor.
No habrá ninguna igual,
todas murieron
en el momento
que dijiste adiós...

Música : *Raul Fernández Siro*

THERE will be no one.
No one with your skin, your voice.
Your magnolia skin, dipped in the
moon.
Your voice, a love-soothing whisper.
There will be no one like you,
they all died,
the moment
you said good-bye...

Lyrics: *Homero Manzi*

UNO !... (1943)

A MAN!

Uno busca lleno de esperanzas
el camino que los sueños
prometieron a sus ansias...
Sabe que la lucha es cruel
y es mucha pero lucha y
se desangra
por la fe que lo empecina...

Música : *Mariano Mores*

A MAN, full of hope,
seeks the path that his dreams
have promised his desires...
He knows the struggle is long
and cruel, but he fights
and bleeds, stubbornly,
for the faith that haunts him.

Lyrics: *Enrique Santos Discépolo*

VOLVÌO UNA NOCHE (1935)

SHE CAME BACK ONE NIGHT

Mentira, mentira, yo quise decirle,
las horas que pasan ya no vuelven
más.
Y así mi cariño al tuyo enlazado
es sólo un fantasma
del viejo pasado
que ya no se puede resucitar.

Música: *Carlos Gardel*

You lie, you lie, I wanted to tell her,
the hours behind us will never
return.
And so, my love entwined with
yours
is a mere ghost from a distant past
which can never be reborn.

Lyrics: *Alfredo Le Pera*

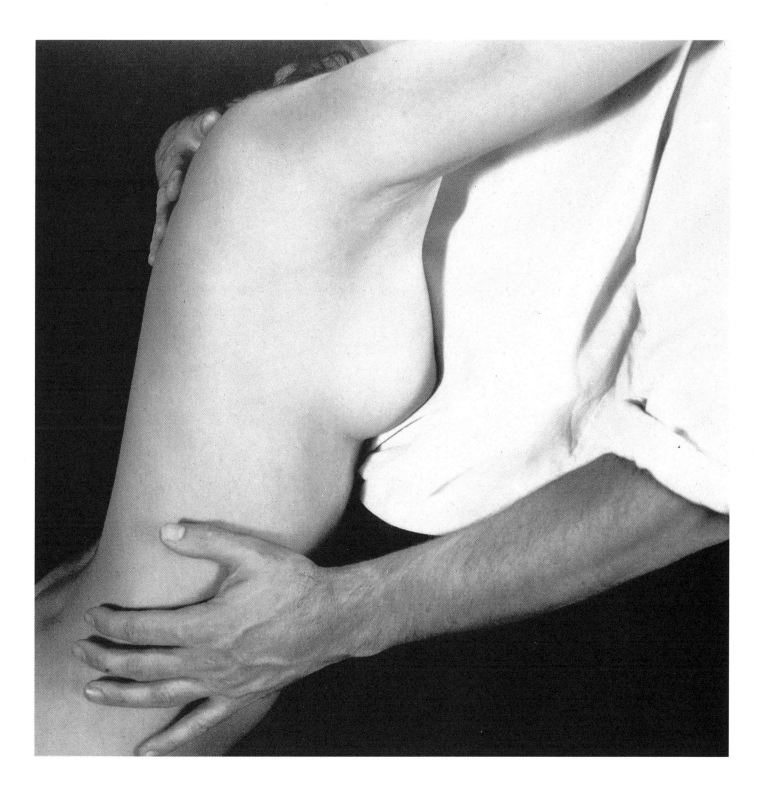

LA MOROCHA (1905)

Yo soy la morocha
de mirar ardiente,
la que en su alma siente
el fuego de amor.
Soy la que al criollito
más noble y valiente
ama con ardor.

Música : *Enrique Saborido*

LA MOROCHA (CREOLE WOMAN)

I AM the dark woman
with smouldering eyes,
and the love-heat
is ablaze in my soul.
I am the one
whose love is on fire
for the noble and daring Creole.

Lyrics: *Angel Gregorio Villoldo*

Con el recuerdo de este tango
vuelvo a verla.
Con el recuerdo de este tango
juguetón que me habla de ella.
Tal vez el patio y el cedrón
que me llamaba.
Y su carita de ilusión
que se asomaba...
Y en el jirón de alguna
linda medialuna, su cara bruna
que me miraba...

Feliz pasaje la vida que duele
como una herida.
Pobre retazo de sueño que acaso
no tenga dueño.
Si estaba el alma en pedazos...
cómo ingratos sus ojazos,
cuando más amor pidieron,
se me fueron.
Muchacha criolla del tiempo aquél...
Tango dulzón y orillero
que al corazón le reprocha cruel
la ausencia de la Morocha
y el viejo patio que quiero.

Música: *Mariano Mores*

In the memory of this tango
I see her again.
In the memory of this playful
tango that speaks to me of her.
It was perhaps the courtyard
or the verbena that called to me...
Her dreaming little face
I would glimpse in the yard...
And in the tatters of some
pretty half-moon, her dark face
would gaze at me...

Happy moments of a life
aching like a wound.
Poor remnants of a dream
perchance without a master.
How my soul did shatter...
when her ungrateful stony eyes,
after asking no more love,
took flight.
Oh Creole girl of bygone days...
Bitter-sweet tango of the river shore
that cruelly tugs at my heart
because the Creole girl
and the courtyard are forever gone.

Lyrics: *Cátulo Castillo*

CAMBALACHE (1935)

¡Hoy resulta que es lo mismo
ser derecho que traidor!...
¡Ignorante, sabio, chorro,
generoso o estafador!...
¡Todo es igual! ¡Nada es mejor!
¡Lo mismo un burro
que un gran profesor!
No hay aplazaos ni escalafón,
los inmorales nos han igualao.
Si uno vive en la impostura
y otro roba en su ambición,
da lo mismo que sea cura,
colchonero, rey de bastos,
caradura o polizón...

Música: *Enrique Santos Discépolo*

THE BAZAAR

Today, it seems,
straight or crooked is the same...
Ignorant, wise or thieving man,
charlatan or good-hearted man...
It's all the same! There's nothing better!
A jackass or a great professor
it's all the same!
No one fails or is promoted,
and the wicked are our peers.
If one lives as an impostor,
or is so ambitious that he steals,
it's all the same if he's a priest
or mattress-maker, a king of clubs,
a snitch or an insolent thug...

Lyrics: *Enrique Santos Discépolo*

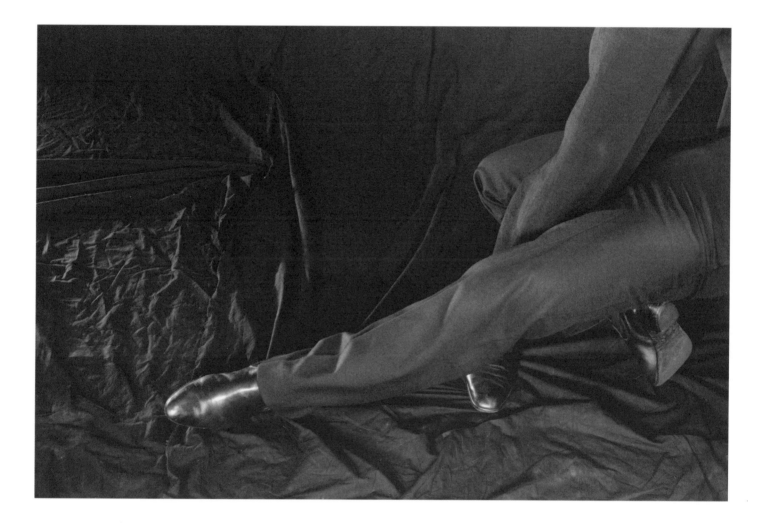

SUS OJOS SE CERRARON

(1935)

Sus ojos se cerraron...
y el mundo sigue andando,
su boca que era mía
ya no me besa más,
se apagaron los ecos
de su reír sonoro
y es cruel este silencio
que me hace tanto mal.

Música: *Carlos Gardel*

HER EYES HAVE CLOSED

Her eyes have closed...
and the world keeps on turning,
those lips that were mine
will kiss me no more.
Now, stilled is the echo
of her clear, ringing laughter,
and I'm wounded so deeply
by this silence so cruel.

Lyrics: *Alfredo Le Pera*

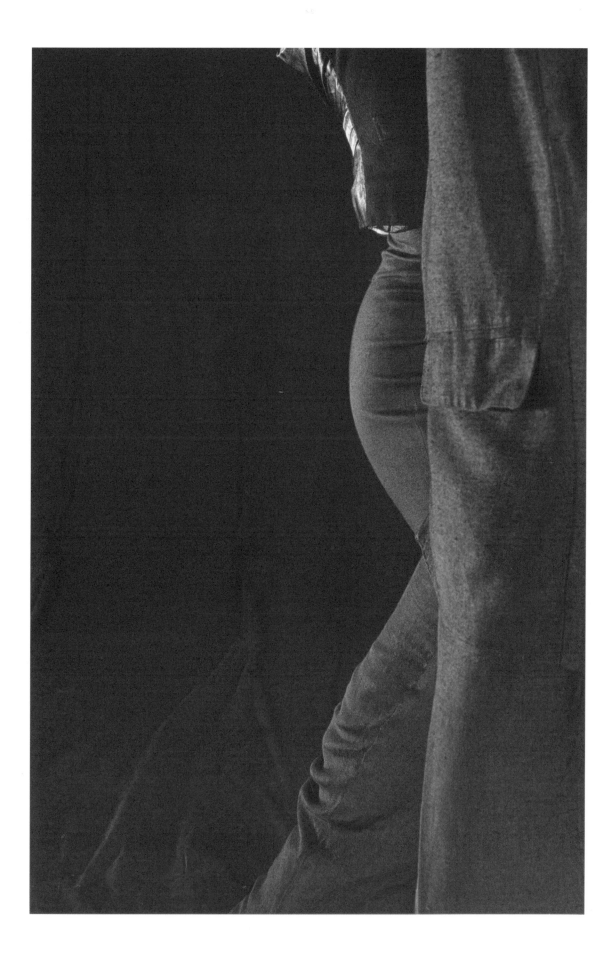

SUS OJOS SE CERRARON
(1935)

HER EYES HAVE CLOSED

FUE mía la piadosa
dulzura de sus manos
que dieron a mis penas
caricias de bondad,
y ahora que la evoco
hundido en mi quebranto,
las lágrimas pensadas
se niegan a brotar,
y no tengo el consuelo
de poder llorar.

Música: *Carlos Gardel*

MINE was the sweet mercy
of her hands
that soothed my sorrows
with gentle caresses.
Now as I call to her
awash in my grief,
the stream of my tears
refuses to flow,
and so I am denied
the solace of tears.

Lyrics: *Alfredo Le Pera*

POR UNA CABEZA

(TANGO-CANCIÓN) (1935)

[WINNING] BY A HEAD

(TANGO SONG)

Por una cabeza,
metejón de un día
de aquella coqueta
y burlona mujer,
que al jurar sonriendo,
el amor que está mintiendo,
quema en una hoguera
todo mi querer.

Por un cabeza,
todas las locuras.
Su boca que besa,
borra la tristeza,
calma la amargura.

Por una cabeza,
si ella me olvida
qué importa perderme
mil veces la vida,
para qué vivir.

Música: *Carlos Gardel*

I win by a head, a one-day
thunderbolt,
that gay and flirty babe
who, by smiling as she swears
to a love that is a lie,
burns all my love on a blazing
bonfire.

I win by a head
all the madness,
the kisses from her lips
erase all my sadness
and soothe all bitterness.

I win by a head,
if she forgets me
what do I care,
if I lose my life
a thousandfold,
what is there to live for...?

Lyrics: *Alfredo Le Pera*

ADIÓS MUCHACHOS (1927)   GOODBYE, FRIENDS

ACUDEN a mi mente
recuerdos de otros tiempos,
de los bellos momentos
que antaño disfruté
cerquita de mi madre,
santa viejita,
y de mi noviecita
que tanto idolatré.

Se acuerdan que era hermosa,
más bella que una diosa,
y que ebrio yo de amor
le di mi corazón;
mas el Señor, celoso
de sus encantos,
hundiéndome en el llanto
se la llevó.

Música: *Julio César Sanders*

MEMORIES of time gone by
surface in my mind,
of special moments
enjoyed in times of yore
close to my dear mother,
little saintly lady,
and my young fiancee
I loved and worshipped so.

You'll remember she was pretty,
much fairer than a goddess,
and I, madly in love,
I gave her my heart;
but God, jealous
of her charms
plunging me in tears
took her from me.

Lyrics: *César Vedani*

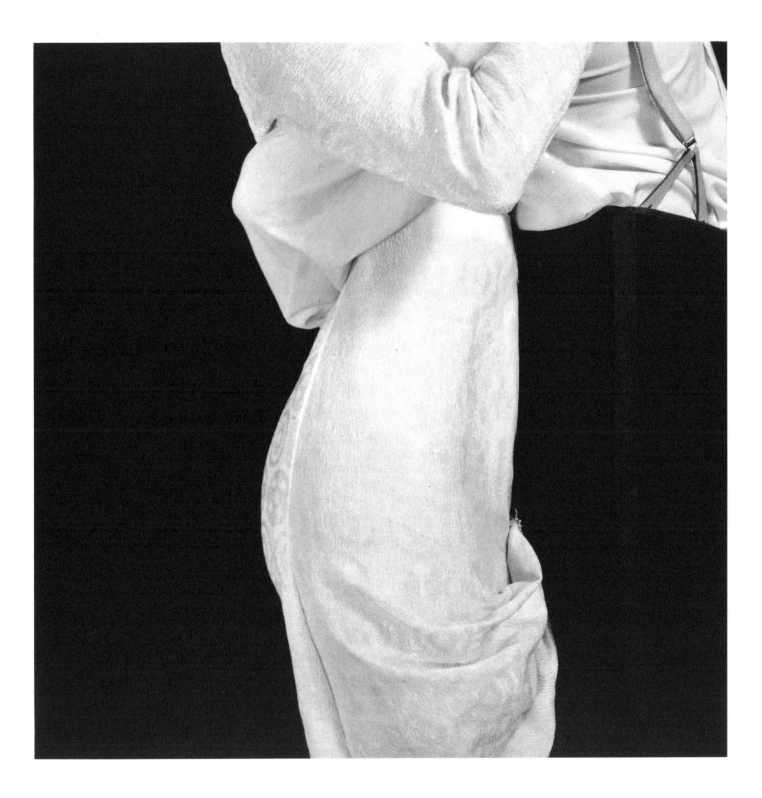

CAFETÍN DE BUENOS AIRES   A BUENOS AIRES CAFÉ

(1948)

DE chiquilín te miraba de afuera

como a esas cosas que nunca

se alcanzan:

la ñata contra el vidrio,

en un azul de frío,

que solo fue después, viviendo,

igual al mío...

Como una escuela de todas

las cosas,

ya de muchacho me diste entre

asombros:

el cigarrillo, la fe en mis sueños

y una esperanza de amor.

Música: *Mariano Mores*

As a kid I looked in from the

outside

as I would at things beyond my

reach:

my nose against the window,

blue like the cold

that I would later know

as I lived my life...

Like a school for everything,

as a boy you already amazed me:

with cigarettes...

with faith in my dreams,

and the hope of love.

Lyrics: *Enrique Santos Discépolo*

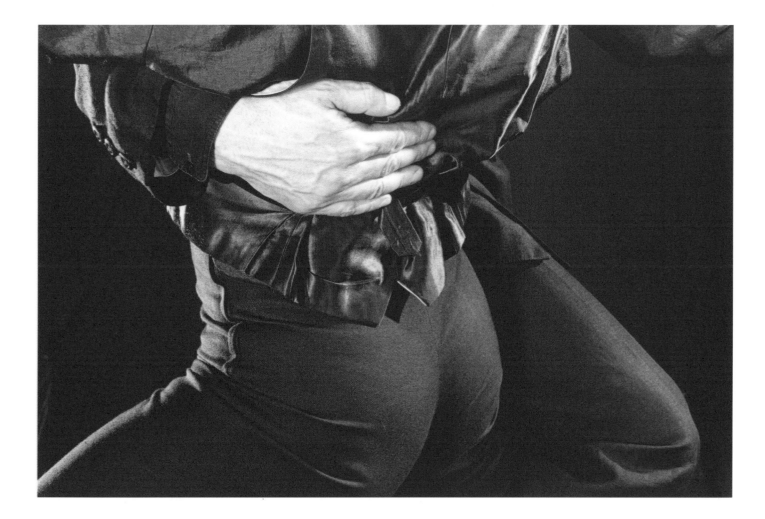

AL COMPÁS DEL CORAZÓN
(1942)

LATE un corazón porque he
de verte nuevamente:
miente mi soñar porque
regresas lentamente.
Late un corazón...
me parece verte
regresar con el adiós.

Y al volver, gritarás tu horror...
El ayer, el dolor, la nostalgia...
Pero al fin, bajarás la voz
y atarás tu ansiedad de distancias.
Y sabrás porqué late un corazón
al decir: qué feliz...
Y un compás, y un compás de amor,
unirá para siempre el adiós.

Música: *Domingo Serafín Federico*

RHYTHM OF THE HEART

MY heart throbs because
I'll see you again;
my dream is lying because
too slowly you return.
A heart throbs...
I think I see you
coming back with this adiós.

And as you return, you shall cry
your horror...
The past, the pain and the longing...
But finally, you'll lower your voice
and check your anxiety born far away.
And you'll know why a heart throbs,
it's enough to say: happy days...
And a rhythm, a rhythm of love,
adiós.

Lyrics: *Homero Expósito*

CANCION DESESPERADA
(1945)

SONG OF DESPAIR

¿ POR qué
me enseñaron a amar,
si es volcar sin sentido
los sueños al mar ?
Si el amor,
es un viejo enemigo
que enciende castigos
y enseña a llorar...
Yo pregunto : ¿ por qué ?
¡ Sí !. ¿ por qué me enseñaron
a amar,
si al amarte mataba mi amor ?
Burla atroz de dar todo por nada
y al fin de un adiós, despertar
llorando...

Música : *Enrique Santos Discépolo*

WHY did they teach me to love,
if it means senselessly scuttling
my dreams in the sea?
If love
is an ancient foe
that kindles my woe
and instructs me in weeping...
I ask: why?
Yes! Why did they teach
me to love,
if loving you killed my love?
What a cruel joke to give all for
nothing
and at the close of a farewell
to awaken in tears...

Lyrics: *Enrique Santos Discépolo*

AL COMPÁS DEL CORAZÓN
(1942)

RHYTHM OF THE HEART

YA verás, amor,
qué feliz serás...
¿Oyes el compás?
Es el corazón...
Ya verás qué dulces son las horas
del regreso,
ya verás qué dulces los reproches y
los besos.
Ya verás, amor...
qué felices horas
al compás del corazón.

Música : *Domingo Serafín Federico*

YOU'LL see my love
how happy you'll be...
You hear this rhythm?
It is this heart....
You'll see how sweet the hours
of my return,
you'll see how sweet
the rebukes and the kisses.
You'll see, my love...
the happy hours
at the rhythm of the heart.

Lyrics: *Homero Expósito*

LA CUMPARSITA (1924)

Si supieras, que aún dentro
de mi alma,
conservo aquel cariño
que tuve para ti...
Quién sabe si supieras
que nunca te he olvidado,
volviendo a tu pasado
te acordarás de mí...

Los amigos ya no vienen
ni siquiera a visitarme,
nadie quiere consolarme
en mi aflicción...
Desde el día que te fuiste
siento angustias en mi pecho,
decí, percanta, ¿qué has hecho
de mi pobre corazón?

Música: *Gerardo Hernán Matos
Rodríguez*

THE CUMPARSITA
(THE SMALL BAND)

If you knew that
in my soul
I still cherish the love
I had for you...
Who knows if you knew
I could never forget you,
if you retraced your past,
would you remember me?...

Friends no longer come
not even for a visit,
no one brings me solace
in my sorrow...
Since the moment you left
my heart is breaking in my breast,
tell me woman, what have you done
to my poor heart?

Lyrics: *Pascual Contursi,
Enrique Pedron Maroni*

¡Garua...!
Solo y triste por la acera
va este corazón transido,
con tristeza de tapera...
Sintiendo... tu hielo...
Porque aquélla con su olvido
hoy le ha abierto una gotera...
¡Perdido...!
Como un duende
que en la sombra,
más la busca y más la nombra.
Garúa... Tristeza...
Hasta el cielo
se ha puesto a llorar...

Música:
Aníbal Troilo

Drizzle...
Sad and lonely on the sidewalk,
this heart is torn
by a sadness of ruins...
I feel...your icy distance...
Because in forgetting me
today you opened a crack...
Lost...
Like a ghost
in the shadows,
the more I seek her, the more I call her.
Drizzle... And sadness...
Even the sky
has started to cry...

Lyrics: *Roberto Fontaine,*
Juan A. Collazo

SOLEDAD (1934)

En la doliente sombra
de mi cuarto, al esperar
sus pasos que quizas no volverán,
a veces me parece que ellos
detienen su andar
sin atreverse luego a entrar.
Pero no hay nadie y ella no viene,
es un fantasma que crea mi ilusión.
Y que al desvanecerse va dejando
su visión,
cenizas en mi corazón.

Música : *Carlos Gardel*

SOLITUDE

In the sorrowful gloom
of my room, waiting for footsteps
that perchance will not return;
sometimes it seems they linger,
not daring to come in.
But no one is there,
nor does she come,
it's an illusion of my dreams.
And as it vanishes,
her vision leaves behind,
only ashes in my heart.

Lyrics: *Alfredo Le Pera*

EL PATIO DE LA MOROCHA
(1951)

FELIZ pasaje la vida que duele
como una herida.
Pobre retazo de sueño que acaso
no tenga dueño.
Si estaba el alma en pedazos...
cómo ingratos sus ojazos,
cuando más amor pidieron.
se me fueron.
Muchacha criolla del tiempo aquél...
Tango dulzón y orillero
que al corazón le reprocha cruel
la ausencia de la Morocha
y el viejo patio que quiero.

Música: *Mariano Mores*

CREOLE COURTYARD

HAPPY moments of a life
aching like a wound.
Poor remnants of a dream
perchance without a master.
How my soul did shatter...
when her ungrateful stony eyes,
after asking no more love,
took flight.
Oh Creole girl of bygone days...
Bitter-sweet tango of the river shore
that cruelly tugs at my heart
because the Creole girl
and the courtyard are forever gone.

Lyrics: *Cátulo Castillo*

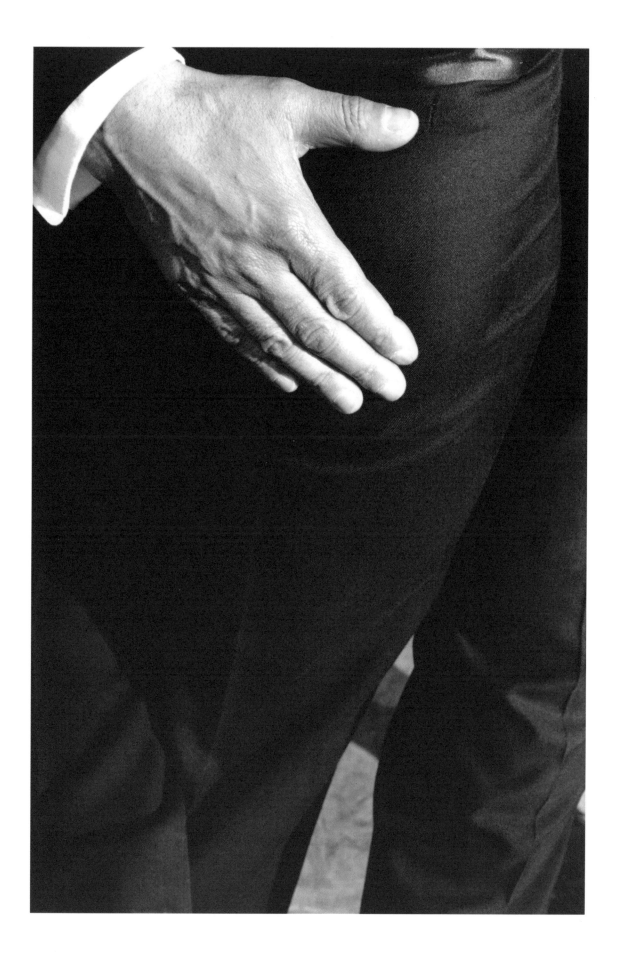

AL COMPÁS DEL CORAZÓN
(1942)

Y al volver, gritarás tu horror...
El ayer, el dolor, la nostalgia...
Pero al fin, bajarás la voz
y atarás tu ansiedad de distancias.
Y sabrás porqué late un corazón
al decir : qué feliz...
Y un compás, y un compás de amor,
unirá para siempre el adiós.

Música : *Domingo Serafín Federico*

RHYTHM OF THE HEART

And as you return, you shall cry
your horror...
The past, the pain and the longing...
But finally, you'll lower your voice
and check your anxiety born far away.
And you'll know why a heart throbs,
it's enough to say: happy days...
And a rhythm, a rhythm of love,
will for ever unite this adiós.

Lyrics: *Homero Expósito*

EL PATIO DE LA MOROCHA
(1951)

CON el recuerdo de este tango
vuelvo a verla.
Con el recuerdo de este tango
juguetón que me habla de ella.
Tal vez el patio y el cedrón
que me llamaba.
Y su carita de ilusión
que se asomaba...
Y en el jirón de alguna
linda medialuna, su cara bruna
que me miraba...

Música: *Mariano Mores*

CREOLE COURTYARD

IN the memory of this tango
I see her again.
In the memory of this playful
tango that speaks to me of her.
It was perhaps the courtyard
or the verbena that called to me...
And her dreaming little face
I would glimpse in the yard...
And in the tatters of some
pretty half-moon, her dark face
would gaze at me...

Music: *Mariano Mores*
Lyrics: *Cótulo Castillo*

Viene haciendo sentir su regreso porque nunca tuvo que marcharse, ni mudar de pie o de traje. Nacío desgajado de la milonga, pero también del tango andaluz, la habanera y el candomblé que eran los bailes del arrabal ríoplatense a fines del siglo pasado.

Nacío para bailar abrazados, para festejar la mezcla de los criollos con el aluvión de emigrantes europeos que buscarón en aquel Sur querencias nuevas. Sus instrumentos : la guitarra, el piano, violines, bajos, y el bandoneón que parece serle propio y exclusivo a perpetuidad.

Fue antes baile que canto. Después "subio de los pies a la boca" con Carlos Gardel. Aunque la música ya había encontrado formas perdurables que la hicieran universal en Madrid, Paris, Londres, Barcelona, Nueva York... Como setas crecierón las academias de tango, la moda-tango, los tés-tango, el champagne-tango, el color tango.

Hubo una larga lista de cantantes posteriores a Gardel, como Fiorentino, Rivero, Goyeneche... Poetas como Discépolo, Manzi, Castillo, Exposito... Directores orquestales como Canaro, Troilo, Pugliese, Piazzolla...

Hombres y mujeres ríoplatenses que acabarón por construirnos en el tango un espejo de dichas y de penas desaforadas, una tremenda comedia de lo que somos en el siglo XX, y "que se puede bailar". Sus héroes son criaturas de carne y hueso, ascendidos por el tango a personajes; los altares tangueros, esquinas, casas y bodegónes donde las ciudades modernas escriben sus efimeras leyendas. Alli caben el amor, el odio, la esperanza, los resentimientos, la afirmación de la vida y de la muerte convertidas en compás y en poema.

Héroes y altares, si no idénticos, equivalentes en cualquier urbe del mundo donde se mezclen origenes y destinos. Tal vez por ello, ahora regrese como el caminante que, conmevedor y grave, vuelve por sus cosas. Y por nosotros.

Rafael Flores

Its comeback is being felt because it has never left, nor has it changed pace or costume. It was born from the influences of the *milonga*, and also from the Andalusian tango, the *habanera*, and the *candomblé*, which were the dances of Rio Plata slums at the turn of the century.

It was born for couples to dance to entwined, to celebrate the mixing of the natives with the flood of European immigrants who sought new homes in the new South. Its instruments: the guitar, the piano, violins, basses, and the *bandoneón*, which seem forever to belong to it and it alone.

It was a dance before it was a song. Later, "it rose from the feet to the mouth," in the words of Carlos Gardel. Already the music had found enduring forms that made it universal in Madrid, Paris, London, Barcelona, and New York, among other manor cities. Tango academies, tango fashion, tea tangos, champagne tangos, and the color "tango" began popping up everywhere.

A long list of singers followed Gardel, such as Fiorentino, Rivero, Goyeneche....Poets such as Discépolo, Manzi, Castillo, and Exposito. And orchestra conductors such as Canaro, Troilo, Pugliese, and Piazzolla.

They were men and women from the shores of the Rio Plata who succeeded in erecting for us, in the tango, mirrors of extreme bliss and sorrow, an extraordinary comedy of who we are in the twentieth century, and one that "we can dance to."

Its heroes are flesh-and-blood men and women, who rose through the tango to become personalities: the tango's altars are the street corners, the homes, the cheap taverns wherein the modern cities inscribe their ephemeral legends. In it we find love, hate, hope, and resentment, affirmations of life and death transformed into rhythm and poetry.

Heroes and altars that, if not identical, are similar in the sprawling cities of the world where origin and destiny mix. Maybe it's on account of this that the tango is now coming back like the sorrowful, somber traveler who comes back for his belongings. And for us.

Rafael Flores
Translation: Christian Caujolle

AFTERWORD

Lori Gross

ISABEL MUÑOZ : A VISION

My almost simultaneous discovery of the universe of Isabel Muñoz and of Spain are inseparable in my mind. Undoubtedly, my romantic image of that country was gleaned from readings and legends. A Spain heavy with passion, shadow and light: "sol y sombra," as the well-known expression goes. However, when I was given the opportunity to get to know this country and the work of Isabel Muñoz more in depth, I became aware that the reason for my attraction was the same. Her work embodied directly what I had hoped to find in Spain, in its subtle alchemy of a rich past and modernity.

In her prints, the artist uses traditional materials used at the beginning of photography, although the use of a close-up with abstract elements is more akin to contemporary painting. Platinotype becomes for her a form of painting with platinum. In fact, the process requires the platinum solution to be applied to the paper manually, then exposed to direct light by means of a negative having the same size as the photo itself.

Her preferred subjects are resolutely Spanish and her style is marked by a character that can only be described as Latin. Isabel Muñoz uses platinotype in a completely unusual way. She accentuates the intensity of the blacks and the luminosity of the whites, "sol y sombra." The tonal richness achieved by this process could not be obtained with silver gelatin proofs because here the colors are not on the surface; rather, they are saturated and impregnate the paper. Do these photographs rouse us to an emotional experience, rather than a surface one? To look at them is already to inwardly experience the passion that is Spain.

Although the central subject is dance, this is only a pretext and hints even more at the feeling of fullness that dancing with one's beloved engenders. Isabel suggests that the tango evokes the moment in which she watched fascinated as her parents danced this most "nuptial" of dances in her childhood home. One could say that, somehow, she fully succeeded in translating and transmuting this feeling, through her own experience, in an adult world charged with sensuality, without however destroying the initial wonder.

Her work takes us back to the nineteen forties, a period for which she professes a strong attraction. Although platinotype was popular especially at the turn of the century and the tango became the vogue in the 1910s and 1920s, Isabel Muñoz's style calls to my mind more the atmosphere of the 1940s. Possibly because it was in those years that her parents, as well as mine, were married. The memory of her mother and father's first years of marriage is forever suffused in an idyllic, nostalgic aura.

Although Isabel's work helps illustrate a certain idea of sexuality, for me it simply symbolizes sensuality and passion. It is true that some images suggest the presence of androgynous beings and arouse a feeling of ambiguity between the sexes. Often the man is naked and the woman draped in her dancing gown. It is not just a simple role reversal, but rather a merging of the sexes.

In her photos, Isabel pays extreme attention to detail. Most of the clothes the dancers wear are old and were lent by friends or neighbors: this was my uncle's costume, this dress belonged to my mother. These very personal touches transfigure her models and allow the artist to develop with them closer feelings of affection, and allow the observer to discover an affinity with the images being offered.

If for Isabel Muñoz TANGO brings back the memory of her parents' first dance, the images leave us with the strong, indelible impression of our own past.

Lori Gross